WORDPLAYGROUND

WORD PLAY GROUND

Remi Probably

ISBN: 979-8-218-08233-8
LCCN: 2022918335

Printed in the United States of America.

First paperback edition May 2021.
Second edition October 2022.

www.remiprobably.com

To Miss Susie.

CONTENTS

INTRODUCTION

Wordplayground is a collection of experimental poems that explore the absurdity of the English language through word association. In this book, I focus on relating individual words and phrases rather than saying anything meaningful. Of course, words are meaningful by definition, so I can't say it's meaning*less*, but any profound insights or universal truths that may be found in its subtext are entirely coincidental.

If you *genuinely* dislike puns, this is probably not the book for you, but I had a lot of fun writing it, and I hope you find it at least mildly amusing.

WORDPLAYGROUND RULES

- USE OF WORDS IS AT YR OWN RISK

- MISSPELLINGS ARE INTENTONAL

- ADULT SUPERVISION RECOMMENDED FOR CHILDREN UNDER THE AGE OF 13

- GLASS AND ALCOHOLIC BEVERAGES ARE PERMITTED IN PLAY AREA

- SHOES ARE NOT REQUIRED

- IMPROPER USE OF WORDS IS ENCOURAGED

- IN CASE OF EMERGENCY, CONSULT A DICTIONARY

WELCOME TO THE WORDPLAYGROUND!

ONE

is better than none the wiser

The stars collide to me
What is this nuclear confusion
At the power planting seeds
Of mistrust

Miss, trust me
I'm adopted
And I'd opted
Out of oxygen

Breathe it or not
You can't rust me

Ground teeth
Grinding my beef
To a halt, er
Topped off
Do not tip off
For the risk of chemical burns

She tipped her nails
And filed the scales
Down to the point
You somehow missed
Me
Missed me
Now you have to kill me

I've had it up to my skin
Getting under my knees
I'm down on my
Here
Aim for the neck
Not yr back
Break for the moon
Shoot out for the cars

We have a blow-out
Blow-up
Blow me, doll-face
Defacing
The wall
Anyway, here's Wonder bread

Idiomatic

Idi-O-Matic
How's the weather up there
In the idiom attic
With the cobwebs and the toys
And the spilled salt
As the saying goes off
On an adventure
Of a lifetime and time again
Yr turn

You turn
No, U-turn
Where do I turn?
You turn up dead

No U-turns here
This is a one-way street
I said turn around
Go around, come around
You can turn left here
Alone to die

Count yr lucky scars you're alive
You survived the fall of '69
And the getting-back-up of '95
55-5555
Ring ring
The line is dead inside

Ashes to ash blonde ponytails
You win, heads I win

And you just lost the game

Maybe you should
Cheer up
Up yrs truly

Get down from there

I don't like yr altitude

Can you do the can-do attitude?
No can do
I can-did the candid
Praise
Because I wanted to lift you up
In the air quotes

Air don't quote
Me on this
Day in history
Repeats itself
Evident

The proof
Is in the putting up with
Me, myself, and eye candy
Cane sugar daddy's girl
Scout badges of honor roll
Call me when you get it
Get it?
Get it, girly
Magazine stand up
For yrself-inflicted wound
Wound up back where you
Started out

What goes around comes aground
Eventually
Run it to the grounded

For a weakling clinging to
One last hope to see you soon
Enough of this

How about that's all
That glitters is Goldilocks
Under lock and keyed yr carpet
Petty crime scene it all already
Already to go-go boots
Got the boot campground
Camping in coffee grounds
For expulsion

We have a warranty to search
Yr apartment for two years
You're under the resting place
Of an ounce of cracking up
The case
The code
An egg
Yr head
Cracked down
To the ocean floor

Under the seemingly normal
Force field researchers
Have yet to reach a consensus

I'm asserting dominance
By wearing recessive jeans
With fake pockets
To prevent pickpockets
From picking yr pocketbooks
To book their first-class flights of fancy
To a fancy last resort
To sort out their feeling out-of-sorts
Until they're out of resorts
And those sorts of things
For those sorts of people
Who have to have everything

At least the have-nots
Don't become has-beens
As in
It has been a pleasure working for you
Because it has not
And the best thing is still sliced bread
So, we'll slice yr head instead

("*Sans*-culottes"?
How about "*dans*-culottes"?
You'll find this joke
In my pants)

I have-knots in my stomach
Can you hear it growling at the moon?
In the moonlighter than air
Up in the air
On a plain white bread
I'm not bready for this

Ready for takeoff
Yr clothes the door
On yr way out of my house
Where my imminent domain
Meets yr eminent demise

Foreclosed until further
Notice me, *senpai*
This is yr final notice
Before we shut off yr electricity
In the electri-city of lights out
It's time for bread

My money
Is on the money
Makes more money
Than sense

One for the money talks
About money
Where yr mouth is
In the money
Makes the world go
Round two
For the show me the
Money
And run
For yr money
Or run for yr life

It's yr money or yr lifelong dream
To be an active participant
In the past participle
Just as you'd always dreamed
Dreamt
Unless yr exempt
From accepting the past
Except for the passed
With flying colors
Flying color-coded flags
Color-coated in hangers
Hanging up the phone in anger
For hanging out
In a hangar without me
Hanging out to dry my tears

On the clothesline

The tangent line
That circles
Back to business:
It's laundering day

No trespassing
Into my Fortress of Solitaire
Or you'll be forever locked
In my FreeCell
That's crawling with Spiders
Unless you have the Patience to escape
Without a card key

I've hidden the key points
From our keynote speaker
Of the house music
To my senate hearings
Still ringing in my hears
To the new year

Do my years deceive me?
Time is only an allusion
To a shared delusion
Diluted with water
From the tap dancer's shoes

I have a sneaker suspicion
That these aren't really my shoes
But I shoes to believe
Until I get back on my feet
And walk a mile in my
Choo choo trainers

I've been training my whole life
For a better station
And I was very infested in my work
As an exterminator

Until I was terminated
For exterminating my ex

I'm exaggerating
Stop badgering me
With yr police badges
And yr search warranty
Is about to expire
And I'm expiraling
Into a deep depressurized cabin
In the woods
That you can search
As Thoreauly as you'd like
You won't find a thing

I find it fascinating
I found it fascinated
I will find it to fascinate
How fascination

Does that follow
Because I don't
Follow along
Or lead, either

Look, all I'm saying is
That I think
All I'm saying is
That, I think
Therefore, all I am
Saying
Is that I think

I ought to be able
To cut my hair into hairpieces
Because this hair won't cut it
Out
From under my skin

I have so many split odds
And ends
It ends up being
A 50/50 split
Between us and them
And
Now
For a commercial break
Down
Calm down
Before the storming
Out of the breathing room
To grow

Tear down this wallet
Chain of commanding
Demanding officers
Office Sirs and Office Ma'ams

Dear Sir or Mammal
Are you a man or a mousepad?
Or a mousepad and paper trail
Trailing behind by a few hundred ways
To diet

Cross yr heart & hope to diet
The hands of someone you love

Tell me I'm pretty
On the inside job
Well done
Steak a claim me
As yr defendant

Depending on my mood
Swings and misses
Swinging both ways with
Yr missus
Did you miss us?
We never left
To our own devices
On airplane mode
Across the median
By any means
Necessary
In essence, I sense

Deception
And by extension
A cordial event

Ask me
To the Winter Formal
It's a formality
And biscuits
But that's none of yr
Business
Casualty
Casually becoming
A causality of war

That's a direct order up
To here
With yr nonsense

There's no sense in nonsense
Not since the accident
Waiting to happen
To have happened
To have hap-penned a novel
Written in recursive
Formula for one
Dinner for too much
Obliged

May I take yr ordered list?
Ordered listless
You're not on the list

So, I'm not listening
To a word you say
It ain't so

What did you expect
From a respectful spectator
In the stands corrected
Where I stand
With yr corrections officer
Discussing office politics
Of the political correction facility
On the downside of town

Don't marsh my hello
Nice to meet yr maker
You can't make this shit up
If you want to make it
Bigger and better get started
At the bottom of a
Well, there's yr problem

Don't make me beg yr
Pardon me, sir
Please assert yrself
Into the CD drive

Press start
To begin
To be gin
And chronic habits
To bits and pieces
Of bitter drinks
In the bitter cold
In he bit her cold sore
Loser

Loosen up a bit
Or eight
To grab a quick byte
But it's a bit too late to start
Chomping at my bitter half

Begging for forgive me
A call
To action figures

Go figure somewhere else

Walk a mile in my shoestrings
And string me along for the ride
Into the sunset stripper heels
If the shoe fits of rage
And love
And I love you like a sister city
-state yr name
And preoccupation

Hm?
Sorry, I was just
Getting my ducks in a rowboat
To prepare for tomorrowboat
And the rowboat uprising

Here's a survival tip:
Just the tip
Of the iceberg lettuce
Pray
For yr survival of the Fitbits
Fit for a king of the mountain lions

The lion's sharing
Is caring, so shareholders
Are careholders

Please hold
Me in contemplation of court
In contempt of courtroom drama
On the tennis courtship has sailed

20

Off into the distant future
Of mankind of a rip-off
The Band-Aid and let it
Bleed it dry

I'll have whiskey
With dryer sheets
Because I don't give a sheet

We dodged a bullet hole
Punch
In the gut instinct
In sync
With the ships
And dipped in chocolate

This chalk is lit
Just a little bit
Oh, I'm a little bit late
For choc
And a little bit *lait*
For milk
It, just a bit
I'm still a little bitter
But a little bit better
Better *lait* than never

It will happen
If you put a pin in
Yr own spin on it
Until the spinoff
Why don't you offer
To go for a spin
The bottleneck
To neck a dolphin
Or is that too
On-the-bottlenose?

Where does the nose go
When the nose goes?
It just goes to show

Until it all goes to shit
It's a shit show
Premiering next year
When they're done shooting it

Doorbell broken
Please knock it off
Or I'll knock you out
Of the parking lottery

How do you ticket
One tick or two
If you want to tock
Take some ticker tape
And wait for me to call
Yr number one phantom
Of the operating room
To breathe
In
Breathe out
Inhale the queen
In
Hale
The queen
On exhale
For half the price
To pay
For what you've done

Are you done yet?
Are we there yet?
Are you done there?
Are we you yet?
Are you there wet?
Are where were we?
Are you aware of ness?
What about Nessie Crunch bars

For cryptid cravings
Or decrypted messages
In yr messenger bag
In the front pocket dimension
Didn't you mention
Paying attention

Paying yr dudes to society
Due to societal standards
Of living a life
Of crime time television

Employees must watch hands
(Unless their watch is digital)
Before returning
I'm re-turning into my mother
Of pearly gates
In the pearly gated community
To community outreach yr potential
Or to outrun yr kinetic
Kinesthetic energy

Do you amass energy?
Is it equivocal about yr beliefs?
Do you believe in God-given rights?
What about God-given lefts?
We'll be God-given leftovers
When we're through-and-through with this

Maybe we should attend mass hysteria
Or read some hysterical fiction
Calm down

You're being historical
Figures
Of speech-impaired drivers
On the road to Victorian England
They have a corset of values
Cinched at the wasting my time
Travel plans

I already booked the shelf
Get yr shelf together
Or we'll miss the flightless birds
Of paradise
Now roll this paradise
Alpha wanna bet?
Bet you can't even
Even I can't even
But I can oddly enough of that

Knock on would you ever have guessed
Never would have, yes
No, maybe so-so
So what if only one
And only the one and only
If and only if you say so long

Here's yr change of heart
-felt like the right thing to do at the
Time out
Come in
The door is open
To suggestive theme parks
And recreational drugstores

Stored at room temperature
Unless the room has a fever

Fever keep dreaming
Dreaming is sugar-free
Of synthetic materialism
Dialectically materialized
Before yr very eyes realized
You left the oven on

I would like to propose a toaster
To Mister and misses the point
To the point of no return
Without proof of purchase

Did you perchance purchase
This purse
In pursuit of a suit and tie
For tying the knot too shabby chic
If I do say so-to-speak

Speak yr truth tables
In the table of contention
Are you content with this content?
With this continental breakfast
Of champions
At the championship match
Made in Heaven
And Earth
As it is in Heaven
Is a place on Earth
Oh, for Heaven's sake
What on Earth
Has gotten into you?

Is he into you
Like I'm into units
Of measuring cups
And a couple more
For good measure
How wood you measure
How much would

A woodchuck could chuck?
I figured just as much
Maybe Chuck wood want
To gopher a run
Into the groundhog
Or is it all hogwash?

I'd love to wash you try
Yr hand at washing yr hands
For at least twenty seconds
Washing the second hand
On yr secondhand watch
Any second now
Or every third then
Et cetera
Et centered at a point
In Central Park
Where the weather is always
Parkly cloudy
With a chance of
Rain, rain, go away
Come again another
Day, another dollar amount
To something
Of the past
Or the now presenting:
The opening ceremony
To our formal event
Exclusively or
Else we'll have an argument
Are you following my
Logic gatekeeper?

The gates will open if
And only if yr ticket is valid
And true
And to tell you the truth
How does that sound?

Sounds a lot like a simile to me
Or something similar
But not exactly the same
As it ever was
Whatever was it?

It's not a contest
It's a protest
Taken out of context

You've won the contents
Of my pursed lips
Cursed with the knowledge
Of God and even
To even the scorn
And level out the praying field

This field cannot be left
With a blanket statement
From the state mental hospital
Spitting imaging systems
Stemming from my mental state
Of the Union Jack
Of all tradespeople

We the people person

Of interest rates
Of change
Of heart of glass ceilings
Sealing the door shut
To shut you up
Once and for all I know
You are, but what am I to do
With all this?

It's a well-known factory

Reset
Resetting the sun
Across the net
To factory defaults
Defaulting on
It's all yr fault loans
On a fault line and offline
Where there are fewer earthquakes

In the wake
And shake and bake
Of Steak & Shake it
Like a Polaroid android
I think I'm Polaroid

Bend and breaking news
Flash
Photography is not permitted
Because indecent exposure
To lighter fluid
Degrades the images

Would you like to save this image
To yr desk job?
Yes, no, or cancel
Unless you can't sell
So, you're fired up the grill
And watered down the stove
To make dinner for one two many
And you eat it all in one byte
Because it's an 8-bit image

Was that a stretch
Or yr muscles will get stiff
As a bored housewife who's
Become a bored-again Christian

If you try to convert me
To Christianity
I will be very cross with you

Don't cross that line
Or my heart
Is in the right place of worship

It's a place of warship
With missile launch at startup
And running in place
Yr item in the bagging area
Of effect
Effective immediately
In yr immediate vicinity

What about my extended vicinity?
Living in another country
Of origin stories
But that's another story
Of my life
At sea you later
Alligator
If the allegations are
Falsely excused

Please accuse me

Of committing a murmur
Under my breath mint
Condition

On one conditioner
For color-treated hair
Free of sulfates
My sulfate is sealed
With a kiss
Of death-defining tricks
Are for just kidding
LOL
L-oh, well

Ignorance is blissfully unaware
Of yr existence
For instance
Rinse and repeat after me
After me
After me

After you
Are finished, please proceed
To cede yr rights
To a free 30-day trial
Try all you want
All you wanted me to do
Was to do away with
The way we do

We do us good
For our health

34

And happy nesting dolls
Idolized by doll eyes
Last seen at the dollar store
Idling in the parking lot
Beside a pillar of salt

Looking back
It wasn't the best idea

What are you implying to my face?
Are you insinuating that
I'm filled with sin
Because I've been vaccinated
Against Nathan?
Vaccinathaned?

Should have vaccine it coming
Over to yr house for drinks
On the house call

Calling all houses
How's this?
This is housing
For mixed-incoming call
Coming right up in yr face
Let's face it
It's multi-faceted

Aren't you fascinated, Nathan?
Are you fascinathaned?
Or should I let you face my
Antibodyguards?

You'll be arrested
For development
I arrest my case

This court finds you guilty
Of third-degree burnouts
Burned into yr mind
I don't mind yr own business

36

Mind yr own business trip
And follow the leader
Of the free world order
Order in the court

I believe operations are in order
Out of order from
Smallest to largest
Where each term is
Blown out of proportion to
The previous term
In terms of service
Serve yr

I sentence you to fragment
Defragment yr hard time
Behind bargaining chips
And dip yr feet in
Into the abyss
And a dip in the pool
Of bloody fingerprints

Er
The fingerprinter's out of ink
Empty magenta
Be gentle
Please, be genital
Be genial
Be genealogy
Build a family treehouse
You're on treehouse arrest
Now give it arrest

Or you'll be committed
To memory
Where you'll serve
If memory serves

You make me feel so
Special
Needs more salt
Of the Earth, Wind, and Fireflies
Right in the face of my
Belief it or not
My problem
Probably
Prolly wants a firecracker
To crack the fire code

Code red-handed
Now handed over
Yr backhanded compliments
To the chef
Of securty

Oh no, my i's!
Now I can't see the difference
Between the square root of negative one
And the real root of the problem
Where x is never
The zero of our story

It's a story about a princess
Who lives in a cast
Because she brokered armistice

Between hairline factions
In a fraction of the time
And a friction of the tame

I can't be timed
To go, please
Thanks for letting me go
In advance

I'm on my period drama

Underdramatic and over the
Whether you like it or not

Show me what you got
That right up yr alley cat
Got yr tongue-tied the knot
On my watch
I'm watching you kids
Get off my laundry
Basket
Case
Of the Monday morning
After pillow case closed
To the public eyesight
To behold yr hand

My grip on reality shows
Just goes to show up late
Better late than everlasting
Never lasting impact
Embrace me for impact
Impact tightly inside me
Sighed me
Signed, Me
Myself, and
Eyeliner

Read my lipstick
Sticking time bomb
Blonde shell of a man
In the mountains
Of New Hamp-
Sure
Why not

Let's try something newsworthy
Was it worth the wait
In gold chain reactions
A cytokine storming the Bastille
In the middle of summer
Like *Les Mis*-summer Night's Dream
Poorly translated
Into obscurity

Obscurity has been
Carefully curated
To cure all types of ailments
That the ailman brings
To yr ailbox
I hope he brought
An *m* for *e* today

Consider the following:
Me
On Social me-dia
Don't forget to like me
If you
Do you like me
Or do you like-like me?

Do you look like me
Or you do like-look me?
Look before you like
Comment and subscribe
And get one month free-for-all
Before the free-for-fall
Of civilization
As we know it
And we know it all
To you

How much do I know you?
I only have my two cents
And I already cent it all
On spented candles
On candlesticks
And candlestones
Can break my candlebones
But words can never dle me

May I have a word to the wise?

A words of wisdom of the ages
Ages ago, agoing, going
Gone south for the winter
Until the box spring breaks
Spring break!
Oh, my sweet summer child

My sweet summer chilled
To the boneless wings
Of an angler fish
Going, going, gone fishing
For complementary snacks
And supplementary angles

Now, take yr vitamins
To the vitamax
Maximum's the word
I have to ask my mum
For permission statement
Of purpose
How purposterous!

Don't be silly string
It's only a theory
Of everything will be okay
Is that okay with universe
Why or why
Not my problem
Got a problem with that
Will be all, thank you
For yr time-sensitive skin

And yr pound of flesh
-eating bacteria

You are, in fact, infected
But it was ineffective
For my affection
My attention
Was unintentional
As one in ten should know
Ten out of ten would recommend
This 5-star restroom
As rest-rumor has it
Has been commendable

We commend yr efforts
To fortify
Forty-five defenses
To a de-fencing match
On the fence between
Forty-four and
A fortified breakfast

The nutrition fact of the matter is
A state of mind over matter
Doesn't matter
Shouldn't care
Full
Careful of yrself

Watch yr Step 1: Of us
Step 2: Good to be true
Step 3: Profit.

Step 3: Isn't a crowd
Step 3: Strikes and you're

Outer spaced apart
Of something greater than
Or less than
Or equality time together
Forever more or less
Lest we forgettable
Tabletop of the World War
Tuesday

On Wednesdays we wear pinkeye
Of the tiger lily of the valley
Of a shadow of a doubt
Don't doubt it, down it
All at once in a while
Away the time
Anyway, the time

Time for you to
Acetone for yr sins
Or something like that
Wipe off the polish
Up yr Polish
Speaking in tungsten filaments
Filled with laments
Is that what you meant?
What you means
With the means
To an ends
Justifies the means

Of a high production cost
A fortune telegraphed
From the beginning
Of the end of
Yr free trial
Free-trial, endome-trial
Tissue boxed in
In the middle of the night
Club
Soda
Pop
Rocks
The boat ashore
Hallelujah

Hallelujah

Did you get my text
-to-speeches and cream
Pie in the sky high
How are you holding up
That sign
Of the timeshare
Did you bring enough time
To share
With the rest of the class?

From my point of you
When I point to you
I make a point to
You know
Don't you know?
Knowledge is powder
Puff
Puff, pass around the clock
The door on yr way out
In the open

On the open road
Does the road rage
Against machine learning
Yr lesson
Yearning for yes, and
Yes, and or equal to
Improviproximation
By proxy, probably

Do you have improbable cause
For alarm bells

Ringing in the new year
Wringing out the old year
Ringing in yr old ears
From ears of experience

Are you fulfilled with dread
Or naught?
It was all for naught to brag, but
I've gone from brags to britches
Too big for my bitches
Be craving stars
Because they're star-craving mad
As a hatter of fact

Quick!
Get the silver bullet
Bullshit
This is quicksilver
Slowly poisoning yr blood
Screaming through yr
Feigned laughter

Laughter all is sad and dumb
This town was dumbfounded
By a dumb founder
We founder body
In a pit of despair me the details

I can't make heads or tails
On the tail end of the stick
Of dynamight I interest you
In some plosives?

I kicked out my ex because
We were consonantly fighting

I couldn't catch a break from reality
So, for reali-tea
I'm drinking brake fluid
Through a straw hat
In a broken teacup
Because we broke cup recently
And that was the last straw

Now, look who's calling the kettle corn
In the coroner of my eye
Spoiled rotten to the cornea
In a cornucopia

How do you cope with myopia
Or my opioid addiction
And subtraction
Of traction control
+alt+delete
My number
From the number lined
In silver linings

A silver of hope
For the best intentions
Intended for a mature audience
On the silver screening
My phone calls the police
Oh, police don't arrest me
For the rest of us

Look at us
We're just a couple of thems
Fighting wordsmiths
And legends
From wordsmythology

Care to join meteor
Showered with gifted
Student loan words?

What for?
For whatever
And ever it's worth
For instance
I insist you assist me
In infiltrating a card game

It hasn't been the same
Since we became
To our senses

You're no harp

Are you calling me a lyre?

I am simply implying
That the imp is lying
Face-down
In the sand
Of an hourglass

Figures
Of speechless
Nonetheless, lesson learned
In less than a daily dosage
Of sage
How dose that sound?

Does that sound
Of music?
That's sick!
That's cyclical
In the sick lick of time
Did you set an old-timer
To go off on me
A tangentleman?

Please be gentle, man
Take my handle with care
To the gentle manager
Without a Karen the world
Wide web
Of Lyme disease
With a slice of lemon

And a slice of life
And a piece of cake
With slice cream

Would you like some
Creamsicle cells?
Or are you iron-deficient?

I cast my vote for iron
Maiden China
Cabinet
Of curiosity killed the catchphrase
Phrase 1 complete
Paraphrase 1 done
Meow you've done it

How do you like meow?
I'm the coolest cat in town
Meow about that?
I'm the talk of the town hall meeting

Meet me at the
Emotional baggage claim
Step right up
And claim yr most prized possessive
Keep it on display
In this apostrophy case
Just in case

This just in:
Time
On the case-time continuum

In a brief open-and-shut space
In space of emergency
Break glass to exit only
Do not enter
For a chance to wing it
At yr own risk and reward

I have nothing to lose
But my temper
I will throw a fit as a fiddlesticks
A stick in the muddy footprints

Will the printing press charges?
I'm impressed by the charges
Dropped on its head
As an infantry officer
In my office, sir

I'm asserting my authority
As an author
To authorize this copy of *Cats*

You cat just do that
Do you own the writes to the book?

No, but I have rites to this passage
And the passage of time is
In the public domain

Ope!

I, um, do not condone
Yr use of oxycodone
It's a little unorthodoxycodone
And it's morphine into a problem
I'm done sugar-codeine it
You need to Perco-settle down
Because it seems like you
Vicodidn't think this through
But you're the heroin of this story
So methadon't ask me
To defendtanyl you
From the OxyContinual risk
Of blunt force tramadol

Hit me with yr best

Shot through the
Heart will go on, then
Get on with it
Get it on
And on
Anonymously
Obviously
Can I make it any more
I can't make it anymore
Any mortal enemy
Anemone too!
Who could have guessed?
My guest, I guess
So, what's next?
Only the best

Stop the pressure plates
Grab a platelet and
Let us play
A tune for two
For just the tune of us
How fortunate we are!
We won!
And the same
Old, say mold
A moldy, but a goodie
Oh, goodie!
Two shoes!
For my two left feet
The pedicure for all ills
Even if it kills me

With kindness
Kind of nested
In my drawers

Draw yr own delusions
From elusive dreams
Of loosened seams
Where nothing's ever as it
Seems okay to me
Is that okay with you?
Are you okay with me?
Are you okay without me?
Are you me without okay?
Are you me with okay?
Are you with me, okay?
Are you okay, me?
Is that you, me?
Is okay?

Okay

I've been roped into skipping
A beat
To the beat
Of my art
Dear to my arteries
As the school's heart teacher
Teaching
Reading, writing, and arrhythmia

While we're on the subject
Verb
Object
Does this make sentence?
Does this make you tense?

How about now?
Are you feeling
Tensor?
Don't worry, it will be
All right triangles
At just the right angle
To see my side of the
3-story building

Let's go for a run-down building
Up the thousand-yard stairs
Directly at the sun
Flowers
In full
Bloom, baby bloomers
Bloom or blust
Like the blest of us

It's a blessing and a
Curses!
Foiled again!
My flood is foiling
My plans
To find the roots
Of this polynomial
Which is bi no means nomial
Nominally
At minimum
Which is at least
Of our worries

Don't worry
Yr pretty little headache
On a stake
Aches and painstaking too long
Don't get ahead of
Cabbage
Read the cabbage patch notes
Shouldn't you be taking notes
Or am I mistaking notes?
No, there is no Miss
Taking a bath
On the taken aback burner

Burned into my memory
How short is yr memory stick?
Does it stick in yr memory?
Is it stuck in yr head
With the aches
Of hearts?

Is it too heart
To take it to part
Of a hole in the ground?

At 12:01
PM me for details
On the side of yr vanity plates
If you don't clean yr plate
With soap and what
Er
What did you
Just say
No
To drugs
Are alike
But I like to think
I can think over my
Headache

Toothbrush it off
The charts
Off the charter school bus
Stop
Sign up for our newsletter
Printed on our newsletterhead
Over to the newsstand

Please stand by
We are experiencing
Technically difficult classics
On rerunning around frantically
Ticking boxes
Off disheveled shell casings
Singing theatrical callbacks
Back to you, crew

This is the nightly news bulletin
Put a bullet in yr head
It's all in yr headshot
Of whiskey

Would you whisk it all
And go double-or-nothing
Will ever be the
Same old, say mold
Growing on the ceiling
See?

Can you keep a secret?
I secrete secrets
I see critical hits

And cynical hipsters
Hip-stirring the pots
And pantsuits
Well-suited for the occasion
-al mishap
As it just so happens
To everybody
And every buddy of mine

Always use the buddy system
Of equations
For the lines of best fitness

If the shoe fits the description box
Oof, it's the decryption bots
At the bottom of the barrel roll
Up yr sleeves
Which leaves me hanging
On the straight and
Narrowly avoided
Contractor trailer
Trailing behind closed doors

When one door closes
The chapter books a flight
Of fancy-assets
Setting sail for the sale ads
For salads
Word soup or salad days
The best daze of our lives
For the rest days of our lives
In the livestock market

Where livestocks are up
To yr interpretation
Of quantum mechanics

Let's play quantum leapfrog
Frogging up my glasses
Half-fully functional
As a function of
An x-istential crisis

Don't cry, sis
Don't cry over the spilled
Milky Way Galaxy
All the Way across the
Universal Picture Show
Starring
The Sun
With special guest star
Proxima Centauri
Approximately four light years
From yr night fears

Relax
You'll be just fined
The pattern
In the sandcastle
In the skyscraped my knees
It's the bee's knees
The bee's niece
And very nephew remain
Would prefer to remain
Anomalous

I'm a fly on the wallflower

Flower child services
Service his
Sir vis-à-visa
Do you accept vis-à?
Do you except for me, sir?
Do you not?
A do not hole
In the wallpaper
Wall-paper-scissors
Wallpapier-mâché
Wallpapercuts won't cut it
Out
And paste it together
Forever and always
A ways away to go away
Go with the flowchart
Chart a 5-course meal and
Mealworm yr way out
Way out there
In the open wound
Wound up so tight-fitting jeans
Low-cut corners
Just around the coroner
'Cause you're backed into a corona
Way back whenever
Whenever we were
Stabbed in the backseat
On the back streets
Under black sheets
A black sheep
Playing sheep metal

By reading sheep music
To my eardrums
Beating me senseless is
More or lesson planets
On planetwork televisions
Of the past and present-daydreams
Dreaming of better days
Gone by
Bygone
With the wind chiming in
And out
Of existence
With a sixth sense
Of dread
And butter
Me up, buttercup
Cake walk the walk
From all walks
And all cakes
All caked in
Makeupcakes
Just in cakes you forgot
To be kidding me

There's plenty of womb
For a fetus to grow
Into a human
And out of a human
To join the human race
To the finish line of succession
Or linear regression
A regrettable exception
To the rule of
Third time's the charm
Bracelet it all out
In the open to suggestions

So, what do you suggest?
Gesticulating wildly
Wild and free
To come and go as you
Please
Keep in touch me
I feel soft
-spoken-for
Or five
And a half-assed hole number

Well, I'm a whole lot number
Than the book of numbness suggests
That beauty is only
A skin-dependent variable
Very able
With just a touch of
Screening
At the top of my lungs

Lunging forward for the word
For the win
But I still haven't caught wind
Of the window beneath my wings

It's such a pane
In the glass
I'm so glad you asked
Politely
Just lite that
In the like of day
And the like
A day in the like
Of the likes of you
Or do you like-like me
Like I like-like you?

If you don't, that's
Like, whatever
But, like
What if
Like, you know
What?
I don't know
About you
But I, for one
Am not one to
Three
For once
And what four?
What's the 4-1-1?
The 4-1-what?

I need more information
And out of formation
Filled out on this form
In the form of a
Functioning adult

I have a briefcase
Of The Mondays
Mourning the loss of
Sunday morning
Would you believe
Yr attitude
At the door-to-door sale
Of a Tudor mansion

Man shunned
By housemates
For housekeeping it real
On the estate
As stated by the dependent
On our circumstance
As it stands
Facing economic collapse
In judgment

Don't judge me
What I meant was
Don't mention it
Didn't I
Now that you
As was previously
Not to mention
The mansion
And the man shunned
From another dimension

Now he's in detention
For calling attention

To the dimensional analysis
Of apples and oranges
Which are both units of fruit

I want all the juicy details
About yr fruitless efforts
To earn a fortune
By building a fort
For the fourth fortnight in a row

Won't you be forthcoming
To my rescue?
That's yr cue ball
Chained to yr leg up
In this conversation of energy
Because you have potential
And I'm kinesthetic
Or is it purely aesthetic?

What a pathetic aesthetic
For an athletic tape dispenser
Wearing suspenders in midair
Amid airbags
Under yr eyes
Just as eye suspected
Such a spectacular result
Tactfully insulted by
A thumbtack

My thumb is perfectly intact
To the borderline of fire ants
In yr pants on fire

Pants, you're fired
For lying on the beach
And on yr résumé

You may resume
What I presume
Is yr Zumba lesson
More or less often
Than nonetheless

Unless we forget
From the get-go
Let's get-going, shall we?
We shall sea
You at the beach

It's closed?
Are you shore?
I don't undersand
A large mammal washed up?
Oh, whale
We could go on a cruise
For ships and giggle juice

Or we could have a picnic
But don't invite yr cousins
You might attract aunts
Why won't you answer my uncles?
That's not very niece
But it would be neat
To be the niece of a fashionista
In southeastern France

Wouldn't that be Nice?

These rosewater lenses
Taste just as sweet
As Everclear
As day

For what it's worth it
Was it worth it's okay
All the while we sleep
Go to sleep it off the hook
Line and sinking feelings
Feel things

Don't mind if I do
-n't mean to impose
The question
The last question
Outlasted is all

All that's left is left out
Out of this world peace
Of mindful of yrself
Get over yr self-fulfilling prophecy

You know
What
Do you
The more you
No
Bell prized possessive
Possessive-compulsive
Disorderly
Conduct yrself

Properly

I hope you don't mind
If I do
If I do
You
Do you?
I do

If I may
Now kiss the cook
Kiss the cookie dough
Eat it raw
Flesh and bone
Sticks and stoned
To death
Do we part
Of a whole other thing

Why is it always
This way, please
Step beside the point
And wait for my signal

Signal and void
Null avoiding you
At all costumes
In the closet
Closest to the tombs
Of deceased cars
Which we visit
On Saturday mournings

Oh, I don't watch cable
I'm incapable
But I am capable
Of wearing a cape
In Massachusetts
Setting the record straight
To the top-nacho chip
Off the old blockchain

Chainsaw it first
Place winner
Winner yr dinner
On a placemat
For learning placemaths

Did you learn yr lesson
To lessen the pain
Of giving birds
A wide berth?

Wide you do that?
Get width the program

You can prograham yr crackers
To do just about anything
Yr heart desires
A filly
To fill the hole in yr punch
And the hole in yr punchbowl
And the hold on to yr hats

Yr hat's on backwards, so

74

Let's get back to baseball
Starting with the basics
The bases
Running to base is the opposite
Of tripping on acid
But maybe both at once would
Upsettle my stomachache

Ouch

That bowl of fruit just punched me
That's way out of line
And they're all out of punch
And we're all in a pinch
Me
I must be dreaming
Of you, dear reader
Can you read my
Oh, my
My minor inconvenience
We'll reconvene at yr earliest
Convenience

TWO

heads for the price of one

Am I allowed to swear?
Of curse you are

Bless this message
Sent from a bovine
How divine
You holy coward

Do I really knead more donuts?
I do not

How can I be of service
If I've vowed to only do goods?

I can't recall what happened
During the Great Repression

I have to tell you something
In a foreign language
It's very imported

I only sing alone because
I just can't duet anymore

I will tell her all about
The high school dance
That's a prom, miss

If two Cates are fighting
Is it a Cate fight
Or an altercation?

May we?
Mais oui

Maybe making things by hand
Isn't all it's craft up to be

No need to ovary act
It's just me and uterus
And the two of os
Are at yr cervix

On a scale of one to tenure
How's yr job security?

Send yr regrets
In remorse code

Thank you, doctor
For yr patients

The best things in life are free-falling
At 9.8 meters per second squared
Because parachutes are expensive

To put it bluntly
Force trauma

Voila! A viola
Has violated the law
By committing acts of violins

We lost the house, and now
It's fore sale by closure

Why is the screen frozen?
I never thawed about it

THREE

cheers for a crowd

We've come to save the daylight
Saving time for something complete
Save complete
Save for
A few more minutes, please

Save me to yr disk drive
Off into the sunset
Setting the stagehand
It over and out
Looking out the windowless
Vantage point
Fair point it out to me
Or not to me
That is the quest objective
Objectively meaningless than
Or greater than or
Approximately sequel to
The film

Rewind
You said this was a film real
But it isn't
The film isn't real
But the reel is the film
But the film is more than its reel

Reel it
In
Great catch me if you cancan
Can't you
Can't you seasick of this is it

Is it?
Is sit me downtown
Downton Abbey Roadblock
Head in the cloudscape

Escape
Key to my heartfelt
Apologies Louise
Apologies Louisiana
Purchase per chance
Encounter spellbound
Spell boundary conditioner
For color-treated hair
Line fracture
In a fraction of a
Secondhand smoke bomb

It's Go Time

I'll have the time
To go, please
Go beyond
The Great Be On
Running out of too much
On my hands of
Time out

It's about
Right on
From time to time
And time again

What a waste of
Rosemary and thyme
From the waste of down
To the very last second
And the somewhat first third
Time's the charmed
Once in a life
Oh, would you look at the time
It's way past yr bedtime
We can finish this some other
Another place in
Just in time for
The time being

I can be at yr house
In a timely manor
Of speaking of
Whichever you prefer

I must prefer to my notes
Taken in note time
But not this time

Not on my watch yr back
To a simpler time of day
Or night
Of the month or
Of the year or
For all time
Until the some rises
To summarize
To save you some times

How many times
Do I have to tell time
With a some-dial
While some die all the
Time's up

They've caught me
Wearing scandals at the beach
To beach their own, I say
I will own up for my own goodness
Graciously admitting
My feet

I always land on my two left feet
It keeps me on my twinkle toes

Twinkle, twinkle, little toe
How I wonder what you
Oh
Oh, doe
Oh, dear
My deer in head lice
With a head license
To make scents
For anti-dandruff shampoo

I'm innocent, in a sense
Ever since I scented candles
For the candlelight vigilantes
Demanding justice
From the man deemed just enough
To convince the public
Who are at the pub
Licking themselves
To achieve salivation

They will be saved
By the bell pepper's pep talk

To the hand it over
Under duress

I got all duressed up for this!
I'm overdressed to the whole nine yards
Decked out in the halls
With boughs of
What are you on abough?

Holly, would you believe
These people are actors!
Acting on a whimsical display
Of affective disorders
In order to survive
On the surface
Of the sunken ship
In a bottle of absinthe
Makes the heart grow fonder
Of sweeter alcoholic drinks

Try not to choke
On yr own spitball
And chain of eventualities

What a teaser trailer park
I parked my carpet
In the carport
Behind the portcullis

I made a portcullist of gates
To gatekeep out
Back to where you be

Longing
For a long-distance phone call
Collect $200
When you pass out
Flyers

It was set on flyer
Better handout buckets of
Water you waiting for?
I've been waiting for ever
For this day to
Come on, hurry up

Scurry up that tree
Or are you a treetotaler?
Tell me a tall tale about teetotaling
Or an alternate turn of tables
Under teetotalitarianism

Sorry for being so
Brrr
It's cold
To the touch screen
Now screening for STDs
And STD-ROMs

Let's watch a DVD-ROM com
During the rom commercial break
I hate to break it to you, but
The cat's out of the bagpipes
Piping hot cocoa through the speakers
Functioning at speak performance

With performative speech
Pre-formatted to fit
The mold

The mold formed
Around my TV screen
So, I TV screamed
Till I was blue in the facial hair
How unfair!
An unfairy tale
Of two citizens
Arrested on the seventh day

How can you go to Sunday school
In the future
Without a pastor present?
That's nun of my concern

Should I be concerned
By a concerted effort
To attend a concert hall
In a hollowed-out logarithm
And blues

Have you red about the blues?
Only once in a blue mood
When I'm over the mood
And under the weather
I like it or not

Ready or not, here I
Am coming to terms

With my conditions
By unconditionally
Conditioning my hair
To cut it out
But if that won't cut it
Out of my will
Who will become the heir
To my grievances?
The world is ours
For the taking turnstiles
In style
And out of fashion
And out with fascism
In runway fascist shows
And run-away-fast shit shows

It all goes to showgirls
Gone wildlife
In wildlifelike recreations
Of their own cremation
Of Man
I Feel Like A Wombat
Out of hellbent
On breaking the news
Of a paper machete

This is Machete, my sheltie
She's good at interrier design

We built a sheltie for the stray dogs
Led astray by an ashtray with
Traces of ash blonde hair

Blondes have more fun
Because blondes have more funds
To spend on the night
Out on the townspeople

Is that a stereotype
Or a type of stereo?
Or am I staring at typos
And are they positive
About their Rh factor?

Oh, it's time for rhesus
Go play on the monkey bars
Of soap scum
Of the earthenware pots
Of gold
At the end of the rain
Rain, go away
And away we go
To sleep

Headspace available
To no avail
Thinly veiled
On a Valentine's date
In the top right corner

According to Dong
The doorbell is broken
But I adore Belle
An adorable orc
And I, a doorbell
Am belting out chords

You ignore me
You're so mean
So what?
I'm not bitter fish to fly
Over my head-to-head
Combat
Please come bat
To bat for our team
You can re-team yrself
Worthy
Of my affected area

This area is off-limits
As you approach infinity
From behind
The never-would-have-scene-it-coming
Soon to own
On video and DVD
For yr CRT TV

What's the tea?
It stands for "tube"
That's too bad

I figured out how-toothpaste
By putting tube and tooth together
For the moment of tooth

And to think
Of something else entirely
Are you tired of leap
Years
And years go by
Some milk
From the grocery storm
Front
And center staged

Stay just where you
Are here
You are
But what am I supposed
To do with
This
Is it?

This is It Girl
You're the Next Big Thing
Of the past yr prime
Suspect
I suspect foul playtime's over
Time to get a watch yr step

Up yr game

It's a choose yr own advent calendar
For the year 2020 vision
As envisioned by 20-somethings
Off about this
Do you get the picture this
A stop motion picture
Perfect
Eyesight my sources
At the end of the year

Happy holy shit just got real
Estate yr business elsewhere
I'm just the secretary
Of get yr state of affairs in order
That's an order
Of gratitude

Happy Thanksgiving up
The ghost of Christmas present-day
Of the dead of winter solstice
In the month of maybe, maybe not
Better late than never
Send a letter
Late or never

Happy Birthday suit
Of armoire
Here's an armoired vehicle
Because we're at wardrobe
Watch out for drobe strikes
And palindrome sekirts
On the outsekirts of town

Happy News reporting live
From Time Square-ever
We'll get that squared away
Fair and square in the eye
Of the behold me closer
Close to my heartburn
Burning bright
Turning tleft
Left of Central Parking lot

Closed
For remodeling clay
That slipped on some ice
And scored a few points
Of contact sports

College ruled
In favor of party
Cloudy with a chance to win
A triptych
To the tropical conversation
On the topic of cancel
My subscription, please

I'm the life of the party
And she's the wife of the party
Working party-time at a bar
-code scanner
Scan you wait here?
Here
Is where I draw
The line is dead
Weight!
It's a dead waitress
Let's way her to rest
In the restaurant

Please be seated
In the fetal position
In the fetal opposition to
A seat at the booth
For the booth of you

Someone will be with you
And also with you
Shortly

Just a memento

Momentum
Um
Um, what?
Ever
Ever notice how
Come as you are
How come?
How are you?
Are you?
Are you sure?
Sure thing is
Isn't?
What isn't?
What is it?
It's just that
Just like that
Like this?
What's that?
That's all
For one
For one thing
Or another one
One too many
And many others
Like any other
Any other kind of
Kind of
Sort of
Just a little
A little more
Little more than

More than this
Or that
Or that one
One
More time
It's time
It is
It is

It's a wash it down

The kitchen sink yr teeth
Into my skintight dresser drawer
Dressed to impress yr
Family-friendly faces
Face yr fearsome beast
With two back to the drawing board
Bored
You're not board
Only boarding people
Only hoarding people are hoard
Only hordes of people are
Bored
Take us to yr leaderboard
Of education
Integrated by parks
And recreation myths

Did you myths me?
Myths universal studio apartment
On the second-floor plans
For this evening
Even though, oddly enough
I've said enough
I said
That's what he said, she said
I have nothing more to
Say no more

Anything you say
Can and will be held against all odds
Even when you remain

Silence!
Is goldfish
In the c-section
Eighth time's the charming
Smile!
You're on camera

Ready to go ahead
Of yr time after time traveling
At the speed of lightning strikes
And you're out
And
As it turns out
The tables have turned out to be
What turns out to be
The turn of the century
At the turn of the sentry
Centered at point (h, k)
At the circle kthxbai

Goodbye Yellow Brick Rodeo

Rodeo Drive off a cliff
Hanging off the alleged
Killer instincts in syncing ships
Shaping up to be there
Or be square
In the eyes

A sight for sore ice cream
Of the crop circles
Overhead and shoulder
The burden of proof of purchased
At yr nearest supermarketplace
That aside for the moment
Of truth or dare to take
A hit or misplaced
Optimism

There's no place like homework
Due tomorrow
Due to bone marrow
Narrowly a voided check
Mate

Lost and if found

Please return the favor to ask
May I ask a flavor
Of the monthly payment
I meant to pay

I can pay it forward
Backward
And psych ward
Psych!
There was never a ward
You win the Never Award
For never

Never mindless entertainment
Meant to entertain
The thought
How thought-full
Of surprises
Surprising to the topic
At hand

All hands on
Deck the hallmark
Of a true hero's journey
Of a thousand miles
Begins with
Making my way downtown

My hands are tied down
To the edge of yr seat
Have a seat

Please remain seated
In a seated position
Of power
To the people
Places, and
Things of that nature

The nature of things,
On the other hand,
Will be handled by Nate
Sure

Congratulations!

Teamworker bee
You made the teeming
With bees!

You must break the spelling bee
Before it's too late
Don't be late
To yr belated b-day party
I made a beeline
A bee lime pie
Because we believe
It up to you

How have you been?
It's been a while ride
Or die trying times
Trying for the first time
To time
For the time being

Speak up, mumblebee
Bees and thank you
Thank you very
Much appreciated
You bumbling idiot

When the showers come

You better wash out
You better not cry
It's a crime in Crimea
River
Cry me a riveting tale
About screws
And don't screw this up
You nailed it
Down on the floor
-to-ceiling windows
Paned with gold

You scored a goldfish!
But the silverfish is quicker

Quicksilver spoons
Melt in yr mouthful
Of sugar-coated in the closet
And spice-coated on the rack

What's all the racketball
In yr court date
Is this a date
Or an almond
Or an almost-but-nut-quite

The food is not quite ready
But it will be cooked
Oventually
Please be patent pending
From the pending machine

Do not kick the pending machine
Or you'll be crushed by its wait

Wait
I'm picking up the paces
Dropping the bass-less claims

Don't drop the soap opera
Operating on the consumption
Of raw meteor showers
And tuberculosis

Consumer reporters
Are live on the scenic route
Reporting for duty calls
Me
Out
On my self-own
And I own you an apology

I'm sorry
I wasn't painting attention

The pain dries slowly
And steadily
And it wins the race
To the finish lime

Finish yr lime juice
Across the finish
Lima beam me up

To no good-for-nothing
No
Nothing
Nothing at all
Swell
That ends well
In the sweltering heat
Of the momentary lapse
In judgmental disease

Disease of access
To firearmies
In the military coat-of-arms race
Riot in the streets
Peaceful protest in the sheets

Pro-testing, 1, 2, 3
Is this thing on point
Is it online?
What about on plane
On a plain Jane Doe
A deer
In head lice
And deer ticking time bombs
Oh, dear
What have I done?

Fun Fact

-check it out
It's a fun fax machine
Gunfiring bullet points
Hollow point-and-click
The right mouse button
-up shirtless
Than ideal or no deal
Do we have a dealership?

We don't ship overseasons
You see, son
Of a bitcoin
Flip a coin to decide
Please respect my
Decisions, decisions

Can you do long decision
Of labor-intensive care
-ful what you wish for
For all I
Care to join me
On a road tripping
On acid bath
And body parts
Of the whole nine yardsticks

It sticks in my mind's eye
It's a mind's eyesore
Sticking out like a sore thumbtack
Tactfully placed on a chairman
Of the boarding school

School's out and about
Of ideas for the summer

Have a nice trip wire
Wire you laughing
My ass off
As of today
I'll kick yr asking price
To the curbside delivery fee

It's no small feature film
Featuring yr feet
On the ground running
In circle the drainpipes
Pipe down
Shut up
It's one-dimensional
A dimmer switch
A swimmer ditch
Dead in a didgeridoo
Did ya redo-it-yrself?
How selfish of you
To do

I don't know what to do list
Do this!
Is a public service denouncement
You have been denounced
For showing up unannounced
To my how's about we
Forget this ever happened

I don't mean to burst yr bubblegum
Butt
How can you be so sure of yr
Cellphone a friend
For all seasonings

Don't sell yrself shortbread
You are a winner
Takes all in one sitting
On yr throne
Under the bus
Stop

Don't be so quick to
Judging by yr action
And an equal and opposite reaction
And there's reaction-nary
A thing you can do

Don't get carried no way
No how about that
I'll give you something
To cry me a river bed of roses
Are red between the lines

Now get back
In lined paper view
You get what you paid four
Out of five doctors agree
To the terms on one condition

You can have yr cake and eat my dust

Yrself off into spaces between
The lines of treason that I
Reasonable doubt it

Everything happens for a
Reasonably priced hatpin
Let's put a pin in hat

Pins and needless to
Say
What's
The scoop out yr eyes
On the roadkill
Me now you're dead
Wrong
Or right on target acquired
Immuno-what I'm saying
To say the least of my worries

Worry not
For I am
Who I am
What I am
I anything
But this old man
In the moonshine
On, you crazy diehard
Fan the fireflies
Straight into the sun

Crash and burn
It to the Groundhog Day

Is the first day of the rest
In piece by piece of cake
Caked in sweat and ugly sweaters
In ugly sweatshop till you drop
The basis
For yr whole argument

It all starts to
Sound the same old story
The same old-story building
Blocked out

Save yr judgmental block
For Jenny
From the blockade

Open up
This is the police agreement
Please sign here
It's the policed you can do
Gymnastics of dynamite
As well, well, well
What do we have hearsay
Can you see
Why I'm on the fencing team?

Sportsmanship overseas
Over sea salt and peppermints
Peppered with mints meat
Me on the shore thing
If you say so-so
So-sewn together
For whatever it's worthless
It's worth its salt
Watered down
Town Hall of famous for
Their role in
On
The red carpet stained

Glass of sparkling why
Not?

Not only that, but
That butt
-ton-down
Tone it down
Tune it
Turnip down
For maintenance

It won't belong
Before they find us out loud
For crying out loud
And clear
A path
-finder's feed
My obsessive-compulsive habits
That make or breakdance
The night away
And away we go to

You should try counting
Sleepless nights
The numbers don't lie awake
In the awake of
Something aw, man
If only
And if
And only if
And when
When in roaming the streets

This place has gone to
Helen, back me up here
Way up in the clouds
The weather up here is
Cloudy

Can a mushroom cloud yr judgement?
Judging by yr appearance
In court
Courtesy of curtsy
Curt, see me after class
You're a class-action lawsuit
Law, suit yrself
Suit yr cell phone
Suit yr cellophane

Have you the cellophaintest idea
Not for the faint of art
Or the paint of heart
With a faint brush
And a feigned smile

You think this is getting old?
Well, so are you
You're no spring chick flick
Of the wrist
Band
Saw
Dust
Bunny
Hop
Skip, and a jump
To contusions
And if you saw this coming
You've got another thing
Coming up next

I'm wearing a wireframed photo
Of us from way back when
We were happily marinated
In marine oil spills
Off the coast is clear
And the coasters are clearer
But the hostess can hear her
Talking back-to-back
To the drawing board

I'm drawing a blank expression
It's a turn-of-face
Phrasing in and out of existence
For further existence
Please call
Cannot be completed as dialed
Please check the number

And send a letter
With at least one special character
For that special someone else's problem

Got a problem with that?
What about milk
Got milk?
Goat milk?
Drink yr a problem with that
Don't cry over spilled a problem with that
Don't drink and cry over spilled problems
Because I'm lactose intolerant

I urge you
To regurgitate
With surgical precision
At the incision site
Set on setting up shop
Selling self-serve seltzer
With cell service

Cells, at yr service
How may we a cyst
On yr internal organs
Systemically organized
By size and shape
Shifting the blame game
Of love you like a cyst

Er, love you like a cistern
It's a stern of phrase
A turn of praise
The lore

Hop in my folklorry
We can sing a folk song
Like "Pop Goes the Diesel"
A precursory rhyme
Before reason
By reason of insanity, please

Please hold
My hand-me-down clothes
Pinned to the board
Of trusted friends

I'm sorry, friend
I can't complain with you
Until the cows come home
To roost
As roost beef
In solidarity with the dairy cows
Who dared to come play
To win
As you have won
-of-a-kindred spearmints
Spearheading west
To pan for golden retrievers
To retrieve a panoramic shot
At winning the gold
Medal
To the petal

When the last petal falls
You'll never get up
Up, and away
With this, too
Shall pass out
On the flora and fauna
Fawning over the overpass
Up the opportunity
To tune in next week
For another exciting episode
Viewer dissection is advised
In this section of the theater
Turn off the space theater
It's too hot in here
In heat-seeking advice

Advice-versa
Well-versed in refrains
Please refrain from
Raining
On my parade float
Or it will sink
In a sinkhole

Are you sinkhole?
Or taken by surprise me
With an uprising
Ri-sing me a songbird
Of parachutes and ladders

I put a lad in the newspaper
He paid for it, but I'm made for it
I'm made of lithographic ink
And lithorally nothing elth

Woe is me!
Woah! It's meat!
Oh, that's neat
So, let's meet
For lunchmeat
In the middle
Or the meantime

In the meantime
Please be kind
To every kind of
But not exactly
It's an exact replica
Of a scaled reptile
In exile
But that's not really my style

Was I wronged?
That's right!
In my wheelbarrow

Can I barrow yr wheel?
That would be wheel nice
And easy
As pie in the skyline
Through a point
Of no returnstile
But that's not really my style
And it's not even yr turn
It's my turnip
Nipping at yr nosedive
Right into it

Intuitively
Indubitably
Doing a bit
Of this and that'll be all
In all that glitters
Is Goldilocks
And the Be Theres
Or be squares

Nobody squares about my puns
Except Punnett

I keep my protons
In my safety depositive box
I keep the key
Inside the safe
For safekeeping

Please keep me informed
As a formality
From a lady
Formerly known as "Malady"
In the latter half of the century

Do you half to be such
An asswhole?
Hold on, I'm not finished yet
I am still plotting
To write a story, but
I'm feeling scattered

I scattered my brain
To the winds
But the wind needs to chill
Until this blows over
And that blow's under
My nose

I keep my nose clean
As a whistleblower
Wistfully blowing off steam
With a fistful of
Steam-powered plants
And seam-powered pants

To see into the past, I
Seep in through the cracks
In my skincare routine

They say it's just routine angst
At the root of my problems
But I really don't carrot all
I said don't stop
Drop
And roll yr own beer
Just in case
In point
Me too
The left
Over and out of sight
Out of mind yr step all over me
Myself and eyesights
Set on you

Please keep an ion my atoms
Especially the alkali metals
And flowers with alkali petals

Forget flowers
I want a carbon compound
For coValentine's Day
Because we have a strong bond
That grew organically
I want something nucleic
Acid, I said
And a kiss on the lipids
Like in my protein-age dreams

It'll be my chemistreat

This is getting out of hand
-to-hand combat
Please combat to reality
I want realty
Not fake tea
With fake leaves
More to be desired

This photo was taken
Before an afterthought

Let me think twice
Before you measure
Once before you
Cut

That's a rap sheet
Tied to the ceiling
Of yr prison cell
Where police are now
Investigating yr pillow case
For fabricated evidence
And sub-linen-al messages

Leave it to yr message
After the tone deaf in one ear
For the hard-of-earring
Earring-impaired
In pairs of shoes

Step right up
Step left down
What a left-down
Left up to you
Left it on the train
Tracks
Tracking chips and
Tricking chaps

Ol' Chapstick

In the mudflaps
The mud flaps its wings
And flies in the face off
Head-to-heading
In the wrong directory

Redirecting...
If you aren't redirectedly
Sent directly to yr frontal lobe
Full frontal lobotomy
Partially kept
In the back of yr mind

Mind yr stepmother, may I
Have this dance
Dance
Revolution
Twerkers of the world, unite
You have nothing to lose but yrself
To the music
Please use yr inside voice
To voice yr concerns
To the concerned citizen
Who lost their voice of reason
To become the voice of treason

One of us is a traitor
Trained in tortured souls
Of the tortoise and the harem
Of harebrained harpies
Playing harpsichords
Until they struck a cord

With my cable TV

The cable stayed friends with
My arch enemy
Who's getting too big for their bridges
And I don't truss them
As far as I can throw them
A party
Till the break of dawn
Until the dusk settles
Let's settle this
For once and for all I care
To explain the plain and simple
Symptoms of a cold
Hard Catch-22

It's twenty-two late
To say you're sorry for the
Wait here
We go against
My better judgment

Please believe me alone
With my penny for yr thoughts
On the matter of fact
Or fictional character actors

Not even once
Upon alone lone time ago
A goatmeal
Got me a
A bowl of surreal
Part of an unbalanced breakfast
On an unstable
Table manner of speaking

Speaking of wish
Upon a stark contrast
About a star's contract
-ed disease
Easy come, diseasy go
Along with the trending topics
COVIDeo killed the radio SARS
Don't Buggle me about it

I'm not bugged, I'm featured
In the newspay-per-view
From viewers like you
Thank you
What a kind jester
Was it all ingest?
Do not ingest
Harmful or fatal if
I swallow

My pride and joint pain
As much as it paints me to spray it

If you get any paint on yr hands
You should gouache it off
With soap and watercolors

Oh, please
It's like you're knot even tying

I've been trying to tell you
In these trying times
Tied to the crimes committed
By omission
To an undisclosed location
Where I've dislocated the world
On the other side of my shoulder

Should've told her
The old story unfolds
Into a couch
To cushion the fallout
After the all-out war
On calling out names

I made a name for my shelf
In the cupboard over the sink
Or swimming pool of
Bloodshot eyes on you
My sights are set in their ways
And, by the way,
I've been dying to tell you

My last words

I wouldn't be caught dead
In a last-ditch effort
To ditch the first fort
And for what?
Well, for one
It was uncomfortable

How do you comfort a bowl?
In a convertible?
Or a converted bull
In a China shop
Till you drop
Dead
Or alive
From New York
It's Saturdaylight
How daylightful

In light of recent events
On the event horizon
Please rise
And follow the lede
Then bury the leader
In the dirt we got on him

Don't tread on mill
Did you see the mill?
Did you seesaw the mill
In half?
I saw the mill milling about
A million times over the moon

If there's a mill
There's a may
If I may
If you will
If there's a will
There's a wafer
It to happen
If you're bready for it

What wood happen
If that tree were cut down?
Axing for a friend

But if you ask me
Only an ask murderer
Doesn't take questions
And we want answers

The victims were stabbed
With a blade
Of grass
It was me!
It was me all a lawn
In a lawn chair
How charitable!

Come to our charity event
It'll be fundraiser
We're raising fun
For the whole family photo

We do not allow flash photography
Or photographic violets
Are blue
In the face of God
All righty, then

All right under yr nose ring
Around the nosy
Neighbors
Under the hood of yr car
Keeping yr cargo at bay
Don't leave
Before you've stopped
To smell the noses

Put on-the-nose-colored lens
Flare yr nostrils at the sun
And the other stars
Sorry, I didn't mean to startle
Over again

I'll be right back
To the start at the beginning
When life began its search
For the meaning of life
That is its soul purpose
Are you sold?

138

Would you rather
I tell you so
Or I sell yr toe?
I'd hate to have to
Tell you so
Long
Farewell
Or on welfare?
Well, that's not fare

A farewell to arts
And crafts
And Kraft's American cheese
Smile and say cheese
And cracker jack of all trains

You're way off track
And this field
Should not be left blank

What's the point-blank
Blanked out on the couch
To cushion the fall of Man
O, Mankind
Thank you kindly
Kind-leave it to me
For it is eye
Can't see where you're going with this

Where are you go-getting
Carried away
In a handbag of milk and cookies

This site uses cookies
Please accept
Our offe*ring ring*
Ring ring
Ring ring

This mailbox is full of itself
Try again during office hours
Office sours
Sweets and saltines
And early twenties
Before the Great Reception
The call was disconnected

You can no longer reply to this
Message sent
From above and beyond
The grave
Mistaken
By surprise
Party guests of honor
Rolling in their gravity wells
Granting and graving
About which wishing well
Granted their last wishes
Wish one of you
One-upped the antechamber
Of secret service dogs?
It's a secret the world may never
Know yr enemy of my enemy is my
Friendly neighborhooded cobra
Don't worry, it won't bite

The bulletproof glass

I lost my bulletproof glasses
But I'll contact you when I've found them
Or you can shoot me an email

Any mail
A knee mail
Get down on one knee mail
To show yr attachment
It was meant to be
A joke, right?

I was just joking
On my own spite

Patience
Is a virtual private network
To protect yr personally offended
Off the deep end
Depending on which ending
In tragedy
With a wave of my tragic wand
Yr trouble will double down
On yr luck
Of the drawn-out story

Tell me a storage
About yr unit price
To pay for a ward
To ward off evil spirits from
Hell, I don't know

I have no clue, sir
You loser
Who, sir?
You, sir
You sure?
Sir, I'm sure I am shirtless
To a lesser extent
To the lessest extent
Of the law-abiding citizen
Of the planetarium
You have such a way with worlds
Of wisdom
And words of wizards
Say the magic world
On the street is

Abra-cadaver dogs
Of war crimes
Against humanity
That's you, man
Pity

We'll make a pity stop
Stop pit
Bull shit
Hits the fantasy
If you fancy me
Fanta-see you after this

I'll hold you to it
Hold me too close
For comfort food for thought
In my personal thought bubble
That counts

You can always count on me
I mean
The menial task manager
How demeaning

What is demeaning of this?
Demeaning of lifestyle magazines
Reloaded with calories
Does this calorie count for anything?

Caloric intake yr time
I'll be here all weakened
From hunger strike

For a perfect 300
In a bowl of carbon copies

On the carbon dating scene
Behind the scenic route
Now I've seen it all
Beef whore
Don't be a chicken
Tend to her loins

What's the mattress?
Are you trespassing up
The opportunity
Cost?

Accosted?
It'll cost you
The fee is *fi fo fum*
Have you seen my *fum* drive?
What about my drum five?
Or my dumb thrive?
Dumb roll, please...
Da Ta
It's Inform Ation
Interpreted
By an intrepid interpreter
In trepidation

You can take me out
I'm a loan
And you have my interest

How interesting
Operation
Ivy League
Of Legendary status
Updates

Save the data!
We're engaging
Yr reaction
To our discovery
Of dis cover-up

You're up to yr knees
In nephews
Who lit the fuse
Dot net

Don't get caught
In the network error
You might catch
An errorborne virus

Everyone's a critical error
Of my one-way street signs

All signs point to yesterday
But that's yesterday's newsflash

No flash photography
But isn't this a flash-on show?

No, it's a symphony
Let's get this show on the road
To joy

There's no shame in losing
Yr marbles
On a marble floor
How marbelous
A collection of cat's eye of the tiger lily
Of the valley of the shadow of death
Of the author of the book of life
Of the party of six of hearts
Of gold
Of course
Of action

What of it?

And what of the floor show?
The floor must show on
It just goes to show
Show it goes

And just where do you think you're
Going so soon
To the show me what you
Got to be kidding me

Just kidding
I'm only humanoid
Diagnosed with humanoia
Diag-nosed with sinusitis
And high-functioning sinusoids
It's a sine of things to come
On
Do you really think

The literal agenda
Is to take everything
Liberally

What an outrageous claim
To fame
And fortune-tell-all tales
Of inconvenient lies
And little white truths

Have you forgotten how
The west was wanderlust
For life, liberty, and the
Fur suit of happiness
Suit yrselfishness
Something sells fishy

It's the fish merchant
Of course, they're sellfish
At the market on the coast
Is clear

The ghost is clearly beloved
By all we know
Has fallen flat
As a pancake split
Split in tuna
Sandwhich one of you was it?
Was it *yoo-hoo!*
Did the deed to my house
Of cardstock exchange

Don't change a thingamajig
The thingamajig is up
For debate
Strategies
In the stratosphere
Of influence
Speaking influently

Speaking of witch,
Hazel

We're on cloud 9-1-1

Too many
Times New Romance
Language credits
Where credit is due
To a misunderstanding
Understanding
Do you understand me?

I'm a cardboard cutout
Cut out of my will
To live
And let diamond
In the rough and tumble dry
Low
And hang me up, too
Too dry to dry my tears
Tears
Tears you up inside
And out
In the roughly a mile away

Let's go swimmingly
In our own filthy rich
Oh, that's rich
In vitamins and mineral spirits

Do you even lift yr spirits?
Do free spirits even lift yr spirits?
Lift yr spirited away
Away to go, asshole
Hold on

Hold up
Hold out yr handle with care

Carry on, carry on
Nothing to see you later
See you later on time to go home
Go home

Yr house is ware?

What makes yr house a home?
What makes a mouse a gnome?
Do you need gnomeowner's insurance?
What about no moaner's insurance
For people who are really quiet during sex?

Go home, you're drunk
On the range of possibilities
Where the heart beats per minute
It'll only take a minute
Of yr matter of time
In the wrong place at the wrong time zone
Depleting the time zone layer
I'll talk to you layer

Home is where the hard-earned
Living in the fast lane closed ahead
Ahead of the curveball
Acurve of the headball
Aball of the curvehead
Aball of the headcurve
Acurve of ballhead

Ahead of the ballcurve
In a formal ball game
Of American footgown

I don't know one cares
Where this is heading south
On a beach in Florida
In or out of Key
West
And another quarter West
Before the half-step up
To C sharp
I need my glasses
Raised
To the mixolydian behind the bar

Let's raise the bar
Or an eyebrow
To make it highbrow
Say hi, brow
My brow line is online
I can browse
Through my eyebrowser
Wow

I Wi with my little Fi
Something that starts with the letter
Go
Let her go
To the letterpress conference
Let her press
Next

152

To confer
With her selection
And we will send a confirmation
To select the next
Not the first
Impressionists

I'm not impressed
By modern art
In the modern age of
Exploitation
Of the working
This isn't working
It's a work-in-processed food
For thought processes
For prospective buyers
And sell-outs

I'll see my self-out

Props to you

And boolprops to true
Unless you're feeling a little fuzzy

Girls just want to have fuzz
What's all the fuzz about?
Are the fees fuzzing around?
This fee won't hurt you
It's just a fumblefee
Feeding on flowers
In my field of fission

The confusion of atoms
In the sun's core values
Can be evaluated by
An expression
But we won't be expressing charges
On the charged particles
Of any particular article of clothing

Please make yr clothing statements
On the mental state bureau
And I will drawer my own conclusions
One way or the other
Or the other one-way street

Wait to go away
To go to a two-way
To look both waysides
On the sidelines in the sand aside
Stand asideways
A little ways away

Waste away at the waist
Or waist a little time with me

I built a tree fort
Come tree for yrself
I'll read yr duali-tea leaves
From the duali-tree of life
In this life and the next of kin
Kind of akin to kindred spirits
To keep yr spirits up in a tree

Do you have a crush on my spirits?
Do you have crushed my spirits?
My wine and spearmints
With spear hints of pepper
And cheermints
At the pepper rally
The pep really happened
As it so happens
I'm so happening to see you
If you happened and you know it
If you happened to know

Would you happen to have a habit?
If you have a habit, you havit
But I am just not having it
Habit yr way
In yr natural havitat

Have at it
Have a tit
For tat's all, folks

ABOUT THE AUTHOR

Remi was born in Nashua, New Hampshire on a Wednesday in 1996. In addition to writing poetry and short stories, they enjoy drawing and painting, attempting to understand the human condition, and making word collages out of junk mail. They graduated from the Art Academy of Cincinnati in 2020 with a Bachelor of Fine Arts in Creative Writing and Illustration, but that's just a formality. They live in Cincinnati with their husband and two cats.

www.ingramcontent.com/pod-product-compliance
Lightning Source LLC
Chambersburg PA
CBHW010334150726
47988CB00022BA/3515